MW00880879

The Teenage Bucket List

250 Things to Do Before You Turn 18

Tammy Mitchell

The Teenage Bucket List

1. Make a big piece of art on a canvas for your room. It can be a painting, a college, crayon melt art, or anything else.

2. Find a designer piece of clothing in a thrift store.

3. Learn to skateboard/longboard.

4. Start a personal library. There are tons of great places to get amazing books for cheap. Scour thrift stores and used bookstores for hardcover copies for next to nothing. Surround yourself with books. Start your library now.

5. Attend a skating party at a roller rink. You may fall on your butt a million times but you'll have a blast. Be sure to participate in all the games, especially roller limbo.

6. Volunteer at a soup kitchen. They can always use a pair of hands year round, not just during the holidays.

7. Learn to do a cartwheel. (You might want to practice on mats or grass in case you fall a few times first.)

8. Carve your initials into a tree.

9. Learn to do your own laundry. Sort it into piles (you don't want your whites to turn pink!) and ask for help if you've never used a washing machine before. You'll be glad you learned early when you head off to college.

10. Watch a meteor shower.

11. Go to the school dance with a group of friends instead of a date. Take each other out to dinner and snap pictures before the dance then hit the dance floor together and rock out.

12. Go to a midnight showing of The Rocky Horror Picture Show. Dressed up, of course. Be sure to rehearse your lines before going so you can participate!

13. Go to a drive-in movie theater.

14. Find a healthy way to blow off steam. Take a kickboxing class or go running. Learn to channel negative feelings into something productive.

15. Clean out your closet once a year. If you haven't worn it in 6 months, donate it to a shelter or thrift store.

16. Audition for your school's talent show.

17. Buy a planner and use it. Write down every assignment. All the reading that's due and all of your homework down to the smallest worksheet.

18. Solve a Rubik's cube. (It's not as hard as you think!)

19. Start a savings account at the bank. Save a thousand dollars by your 18th birthday. You'll thank yourself

later for having a safety net of cash.

20. Take a dance class.

21. Write a novel during National Novel Writing Month (NaNoWriMo). You can

22. Make a collage from old magazines. Whether it's just the cover of your notebook or a whole wall, create something inspiring to look at.

23. Prank call a friend.

24. Quit a bad habit. Biting your nails? Leaving your clothes on the floor? Change it!

25. Have a gigantic water balloon or squirt gun fight in the summer time.

26. Listen more.

27. Drive somewhere out into the country that there aren't many lights or light pollution to cover the stars. Bring a star map and map out the constellations or just lay out a blanket and look up at the universe. If it's a really clear night and there's not a lot of light, you might even be able to see the Milky Way.

28. Start a windowsill garden for herbs or flowers, something small to brighten your day.

29. Go to a game/meet for each sport at your school.

30. Change your hair dramatically. Dye it a completely different color. Get a pixie cut. Do something new. Hair can always grow back.

31. Eat whipped cream right from the can.

32. Start telling your parents that you love them. They might anger you or tell you that you can't do some of the things you'd like to but they're doing it because they love you. They won't be around forever. Remind them that you love them, even if you don't like them all the time.

33. Race your friends at a go-kart track.

34. Learn to say "It's my fault." Owning up to your actions (even if it was a mistake) is always better than lying about them. Learn to be the bigger person and admit fault.

35. Go to a music festival.

36. Make your own smoothies. All you need is a blender, ice, fruit, juices or yogurt and some sugar or artificial sweetener for a cool yummy treat.

37. Join a school club. It doesn't matter what club it is, just join in and participate. Help build the homecoming float or plan the meetings, run to be the

club's president, or just go to hang out. You'll meet new people and probably learn a thing or two.

38. Participate in a flash mob. Whether you're dancing, freezing, or playing music, flashmobs are fun and memorable for the participants and the audience.

39. Draw your family tree.

40. Stop wearing pajamas in public. I know, they're comfortable and it's hard to get ready when you're still half asleep but there are plenty of clothes out there that look twice as awesome and are just as comfortable. (Hint· Try leggings.) Remember· always dress like you're going to go head to head with your worst enemy and everyone knows you can't come across your enemy without being the fiercest person in the room.

41. Take pictures in a photo booth with your friends. Make sure each person gets a set of photos to keep.

42. Get straight A's one semester. It might be tough but you'll feel so accomplished.

43. Eat an entire pint of ice cream in one sitting. This is best reserved for breakups and bad days.

44. Get your palm read. It'll be silly and will probably cost $5-$10 but why not?

45. Start recycling items in your home or school if you don't already. Create a place for recyclable items to be stored, find out where they need to be taken or if they can be picked up, and figure out what items you can recycle.

46. Talk to your grandparents. Learn your family history. Write down their stories; they won't be around forever to tell them.

47. Lock your door, put on some really loud obnoxious music and dance in your underwear. Using a hairbrush microphone is totally optional but definitely encouraged.

48. Get a henna tattoo.

49. Create your very own recipe to pass down in your family.

50. Sometimes it's okay to be ridiculous so go ahead and pool some money with friends and rent the limo for prom. Just do it.

51. Do the splits. (You'll have to work up to this a bit. Start with some yoga and deep stretches and you'll be on your way in no time!)

52. Walk through a fast food drive thru.

53. Go see a ballet performance.

54. Wish on a shooting star.

55. Plan a road trip with your best friend. Whether it's a day trip or a week long adventure, plan it out, save up some money and make it a reality.

56. Attend a costume party.

57. Try sushi.

58. Leave the GPS at home, fill up your gas tank, grab a friend, drive until you're lost and then find your way back.

59. Learn to sew on a button and fix a hemline for those moments your coat buttons pop off on your way out of the house before an important meeting.

60. Send a postcard to Postsecret. Sometimes sending your secret off into the world makes it easier to overcome or manage.

61. Fingerpaint. Fingerpainting is not just for children. Let the cool paint squish between your fingers and go for it. Paint your heart out.

62. Take part in a protest and support something you believe in.

63. Stay up all night and go to bed as the sun rises.

64. Visit a zoo.

65. Be able to recite the alphabet backwards.

66. Learn HTML and create a website. It can be a silly blog or something a little more serious but HTML is a great skill to know down the road.

67. Jump into a pool/the ocean fully clothed.

68. Write a love letter to your crush. You don't have to send it or even keep it but just letting it out will feel good.

69. Go a day without wearing shoes. Feel the ground beneath your feet.

70. Wear bright red lipstick.

71. Join a sports team. Whether it's school sports or a parks and recreation league, joining a team can help you meet new friends and get a great workout all at once. Can't beat that!

72. Go to prom. Whether you've got a date or you're going stag, go to prom. It's a cheesy high school event and you'll regret not going. If you think you can't afford a big fancy dress, thrift it or borrow a dress from a friend. There's no need to spend $100 on a dress you'll most likely only wear once.

73. Donate blood. You have to be 17 (or 16 with parental consent) to donate blood.

74. Build a blanket fort and camp out inside of it watching movies on your laptop.

75. Audition for the school play. If you don't make it, there's always next time or volunteer to be a part of the stage crew. The actors are nothing without the crew to help them out!

76. Be up against the rail or front row at a concert.

77. Fill up and entire journal or sketchbook with writing, art, and memories.

78. Visit a college. You don't have to go to college right out of high school if you're not ready but touring one can't hurt.

79. Finish a whole tube of chapstick before losing it. (I know, this one is tough.)

80. Volunteer your time. Whether it's at an animal shelter, reading to children, or working at a nursing home, give your time to someone or something that needs it. Make the world a better place.

81. Go to an orchard and pick your own fruit.

82. Buy a pair of white canvas shoes and color them

with sharpies or waterproof paints.

83. Buy a pair of jumper cables, learn to use them, and then throw them in your trunk. You never know when you'll accidentally leave your headlights on all night and need a jump to get to work or school the next day.

84. Also, learn to change a tire and keep a spare in your car. No matter how small your car is, make room for a spare tire!

85. Attempt a "Man vs. Food" challenge at a restaurant. Don't be discouraged if you don't finish and don't get sick if you do!

86. Get first aid and CPR certified. It's better to be trained and never need to use it than to be untrained in an emergency situation.

87. Bake a cake from scratch. Break out the cookbooks, no box mixes allowed!

88. See the ocean.

89. Cut back on the swear words. You don't have to stop completely but just cut back a little bit. Every other word doesn't need to start with "F."

90. Get your driver's license. (Don't text and drive, please.)

91. Along with getting your license, learn to drive a stick shift. You never know when you'll need to drive a friend's car home for some reason and low and behold… it's a manual.

92. Stop going to the tanning bed. You're damaging your skin. I know, I know, you want to look awesome for prom or keep your "color" in the winter time. Stop going. You'll love yourself later in life for this decision.

93. Learn a language. Yep, that actually means paying attention in French class. It'll pay off one day, I promise.

94. Grow your hair out to donate it to children with cancer.

95. Attend a bonfire on a cold night.

96. Learn to play an instrument. Even if it's just a recorder and you can only play "Hot Crossed Buns."

97. Climb a mountain.

98. Meet a celebrity.

99. Bake an awesome birthday cake for a friend or family member. Homemade is always better than bakery (well, most of the time, anyway). You can make an icing piping bag by putting colored icing into a ziplock bag and cutting the corner off!

100. Write bad poetry. Keep it in a journal and write all the bad poems you can. Don't show them to people. Don't put them on a blog. Just keep them to yourself. Some poems are made to be written and never read. Write those.

101. Ride the biggest roller coaster at the theme park and scream until your throat hurts.

102. Learn to use a fire extinguisher. It's better to learn before you need to know how to use one.

103. Be the only ones in the movie theater.

104. Learn how to properly put on a condom. You may not be ready to have sex yet but when you decide to do it, make sure you know how to be safe.

105. Go to the county fair. Eat all the fried foods you can and go on the ferris wheel. You might want to do the ferris wheel before the food though. Just in case.

106. Learn to cook. Learn a few basic meals· baked chicken breasts, mashed potatoes, spaghetti, and homemade mac and cheese are great easy foods to cook. Your stomach will thank you when you move out.

107. Participate in a color run.

108. Crowd surf at a concert.

109. Find the perfect pair of jeans. You know, the kind of jeans you never want to take off because they just look that good. Don't settle for a pair because they're $4. Get the pair that makes you feel awesome.

110. Go ice skating.

111. Catch fireflies in a far. Be sure to poke holes in the lid first and to release them afterwards.

112. Record a cover of your favorite song and put it on Youtube.

113. Create a chalk mural on a public sidewalk or on a neighborhood street.

114. Get a summer job. Whether it's asking if "you'd like fries with that," lifeguarding at a pool, or working at a retail store, a summer job will give you some extra spending money and will give you valuable work experience that will be helpful for resume building later on.

115. Learn to play poker.

116. Pay it backward. Pay for the person's food behind you in the drive thru or another table's food at a restaurant.

117. Spend a whole day at the mall. Buy a new outfit. Eat a soft pretzel. People watch. Hang out with your

friends.

118. Buy a homeless person a meal. Sit with him while he eats it and have a conversation.

119. Start a club in school.

120. Get lost in a book.

121. Go to a makeup counter and get a makeover. Be prepared to buy one or two products to keep feeling fabulous.

122. Have a pinata at your birthday party.

123. Go to Warped Tour with a group of friends.

124. Participate in an attempt to break a world record. Doesn't matter what it is, join in and set a record.

125. Use a fake name when making dinner reservations. Be creative.

126. Learn the entirety of Michael Jackson's "Thriller" dance. Bonus points for learning the "Single Ladies" dance from Beyonce's video.

127. Dress up really fancy and go out to eat at a fast food restaurant. Treat it like five star dining.

128. Learn to eat with chopsticks.

129. Have a tie-dye party with friends. Tie-dye shirts, tote bags, shorts or anything you want.

130. Win a contest. It can be something as silly as a hula hoop contest at a barbeque or a contest for a full ride scholarship. Big or small, winning makes you feel great.

131. Mail someone a letter via snail mail. There's nothing better than getting fun mail instead of bills and junk.

132. Hold up a free hugs sign. Be sure to give away tons of free hugs. Not a hugger? Free high fives work too.

133. Go to a midnight movie release in costume.

134. Participate in a poetry slam. The key is practice, practice, practice.

135. Take the SAT test. At least twice. Just do it. Follow it up with the ACT for good measure.

136. Build a gingerbread house.

137. Learn to love your body. So what if one boob is smaller than the other, your left eye droops a little when you're tired, or your stomach isn't supermodel thin? You're awesome the way you are.

138. Make your own homemade popsicles. Add in fresh

fruit and juices to a popsicle mold then freeze. Easy and delicious.

139. Watch every episode of your favorite TV show.

140. Ride a mechanical bull.

141. Dance in a rainstorm. Pouring down rain, puddles, and rainboots are all required (unless you want to go barefoot, of course!)

142. Get ice cream from an ice cream truck.

143. Photobomb a stranger's tourist photo.

144. Go vegetarian. It can be for a whole week or a whole lifetime but go veggie. Use it as an excuse to try new foods. (I recommend black bean burgers. Yum!)

145. Participate in an open mic night.

146. Go to a signing. A book signing, album signing, movie signing, anything.

147. Sign up a class in school that you wouldn't normally take. Wood shop? Architecture? Drama? Try something new!

148. Have your first kiss.

149. Attempt to fry an egg on the sidewalk. I wouldn't recommend eating it though.

150. Collect seashells on the beach.

151. Read at least 10 books a year for fun. Any books. Big or small. Just read.

152. Buy your best friend a present just because.

153. Learn to french braid.

154. Volunteer to help clean up a neighborhood park for an afternoon.

155. Do a flip off the diving board.

156. Decorate your room with Christmas lights. It's the easiest and cheapest way to turn your room from darkness to dreamland in an instant.

157. Leave your initials (or your handprints) in wet concrete.

158. Buy a disposable camera and fill up the roll of film in one day. Make a scrapbook or a photo album with the photos from that roll.

159. Learn to walk in high heels, even if it's just to use your hallway as a runway.

160. Find a four leaf clover.

161. Attend a parade. (Bonus points for being in the parade!)

162. Spend a whole day lounging around in bed in your pjs. There is no shame in taking a day to relax and veg out. Give yourself time to unwind.

163. Design and sew and article of clothing for yourself.

164. Go for a hike in the woods.

165. Build a snow man.

166. Learn to meditate and dedicate a few minutes a day to it. Spend some time relaxing and decompressing. You will feel much better.

167. Bake a recipe you found on Pinterest. The biggest, craziest cake or the cutest little cupcakes. Make it a reality. Then eat it, of course.

168. Go skinnydipping. Strip down and go for a dip! (No photography allowed. Period.)

169. Go blacklight bowling.

170. Learn to say "no." Just because someone asks for something or to do something, doesn't mean you have to say "yes."

171. On the other hand, learn to say "yes." Try new things. Help someone out when they ask for it. Put someone else before you.

172. Create the world's most perfect playlist.

173. Visit a strange roadside attraction. Whether it's the world's largest ball of twine, a giant avocado sculpture, or something else bizarre, hop in the car with a friend and go see it.

174. Compliment a complete stranger. You could make their entire day with just a few kind words.

175. Win a radio station contest. Whether you win front row tickets to a concert or tickets to a craft fair, winning is winning. Just call in when you hear them announce the contest and hope for the best!

176. Take 1 photo every day for a whole year.

177. Try a "strange" food. Chocolate covered bacon? Yep. An insect delicacy? Sure. Try something unusual.

178. Learn to juggle. Don't try anything crazy, like juggling chainsaws, but learning to juggle will make a great party trick later in life.

179. Go swimming in a fountain.

180. Create your own time capsule to open in ten years and see how far you've come.

181. Hold a yard sale and get rid of some of your old stuff while making some pocket money as well.

182. Go zip-lining.

183. Watch at least 25 of the American Film Institute's list of the top 100 films of all time.

184. Go to a haunted house for Halloween. (Or a real haunted house, depending on how brave you are.)

185. Disconnect. Go a whole day without technology. Turn off the cell phones, laptops, and television sets. Make like it's 1985.

186. Get a manicure and pedicure at a day spa.

187. Throw someone a surprise party.

188. Read the news. Make it a habit.

189. Learn to truly apologize.

190. Own 100 of something. Whether it's nail polish, teddy bears, or pairs of socks, own 100 of something you love.

191. Make every recipe in a cookbook.

192. Run a 5k. You may need to do some training and prep work but it'll all be worth it when you cross the finish line.

193. Perfect your handshake. No limp, wimpy handshakes. This is a life skill. Do it right.

194. Make drinking soda a treat instead of a routine and opt for tea or coffee to get your daily caffeine.

195. Take a nap in a hammock.

196. Write a complaint/satisfaction letter to a company. You may even be able to score some free swag.

197. Attend a fashion show. Believe it or not, you don't have to live in a huge city to see a fashion show. Many smaller cities and towns have local designers and local fashion weeks that you can attend. Just because it's not New York Fashion Week doesn't mean it's not fabulous.

198. Buy your first car.

199. Let loose and sing karaoke at the top of your lungs.

100. Get some sleep. Don't be afraid to sleep in until noon sometimes or go to bed super early. If your body needs it, do it.

201. Have a shopping cart race.

202. Go see a play. Whether it's on Broadway or a school production, go to the theater.

203. Learn to swim.

204. Make something out of duct tape. (Wallets and purses are super easy and look really cool.)

205. Get your heart broken. Dealing with break-ups is hard and miserable but how else are you meant to learn who's right and wrong?

206. Play Truth or Dare.

207. Go tent camping for a weekend. It can be in your backyard or way out in the woods but just go camping.

208. Play hooky from school one day. Sit on the couch and watch TV movies all day or take the day off with a friend or two and go out for breakfast then spend the day goofing off. One day won't hurt, just don't make a habit of skipping school.

209. Write a letter to the editor and get it published in the newspaper.

210. Rake a giant pile of leaves and jump into it.

211. Scream into a pillow when you're really, really mad. It feels so, so good.

212. Slow down the shutter speed on your camera and take photos by writing in the air with sparklers. You can make all kinds of cool designs.

213. Stop waiting to be asked out and do the asking.

Ask someone to prom or out to coffee. Either way, what's the worst that could happen?

214. Learn to forgive. It may be hard to forgive someone who has betrayed you or done something wrong but forgiving is easier than harboring a lifelong grudge. Forgive and move on.

215. Finish a game of Monopoly.

216. Start and awesome collection. (I don't recommend Beanie Babies but anything else could probably work.)

217. Hit someone in the face with a pie. (Whipped cream pies are the best for this!)

218. Buy flowers for someone for no reason. It can be a friend, a crush, or a relative. Surprise them.

219. Crash a party. (Pro-tip· It's easier to crash big parties.)

220. Kiss a stranger. This one would be fun on New Year's.

221. Learn to knit or crochet.

222. Hang out on your roof. Just be careful, please.

223. Conquer your biggest fear.

224. Adopt a pet. even if it's just a Beta fish.

225. Go to a diner after midnight for burgers or breakfast (they'll probably serve both.)

226. Suck in helium from a balloon and talk like a chipmunk.

227. Go horseback riding.

228. Get into a snowball fight.

229. Dress up and go out to eat at a nice restaurant. You know, a really nice restaurant with white tablecloths and candles on the table. Everyone deserves to spend a little extra money on a really awesome meal every now and then.

230. Learn to hem a pair of pants or a skirt. This will save you so much money by avoiding a tailor.

231. Be able to do a free-standing handstand.

232. Drive around with a "Honk if…" sign on your car. See how many honks you can get and be creative with your sign.

233. Sing in the shower. Belt it out like no one is listening. The acoustics are never better than in your tub, I promise.

234. Go ghost hunting. Pretty much all you need is a camera and a voice recorder.

235. Dip-dye your hair with Kool-Aid. Dissolve 1-2 packets of Kool-Aid into ¾ cups of hot water. Dip the ends of your hair into the mixture and keep it there for 30 minutes. After your 30 minutes are up, rinse your hair with lukewarm water. Be prepared to use dark colored towels because Kool-Aid will stain everything!

236. Plant a tree.

237. Drink hot chocolate with extra marshmallows on a cold day.

238. Bury someone in the sand. (Or have someone bury you in the sand.)

239. Attend a professional sporting event. It can be any sport· basketball, football, baseball, anything. Just go to one and cheer on your team.

240. Have your own lemonade stand with homemade lemonade.

241. Go on a picnic. Basket, plaid blanket, and all.

242. Do a foreign exchange program for six months and explore a new country.

243. Leave a note in a library book for the next person who reads that book to find.

244. Order dessert first at a restaurant. Life's too short to miss out on cheesecake.

245. Win a giant stuffed animal playing a carnival game.

246. Graduate. You need that piece of paper to tell you that you survived high school. You need it. So keep going! Yes, high school is petty and boring sometimes but just keep pushing forward.

247. Babysit for a family friend or a neighbor. There are babysitting classes you can take if you're nervous about the responsibility but just play with the kids, keep them safe, and don't destroy the house and you'll be a great success.

248. Eat food from a food cart or truck. You'd be surprised how many types of food you can try from carts and trucks in your area.

249. Send a message in a bottle. Leave your email address in the message for whoever finds it to contact you.

250. Create and complete a high school scrapbook to remember everything you did.

About The Author

Tammy Mitchell is a writer who loves coming up with new ways to enjoy life to the fullest. Find more fun things to do at tammy-mitchell.com

CPSIA information can be obtained
at www.ICGtesting.com
Printed in the USA
BVHW040849271018
530902BV00007B/10/P